OXFORD
UNIVERSITY PRESS

Training Like an Athlete

Nash Kramer

Contents

Introduction

Would you like to kick a football like David Beckham, or hit a tennis ball as hard as Serena Williams?

Many people think that they have become the best in the world at their sports because they are such good athletes. An athlete is a person who is good at athletic sports like running and jumping. They are fit and strong.

Find out what makes each of the people in this book such a good athlete.

David Beckham

Serena Williams

Tiger Woods

Ian Thorpe

David Beckham
Footballer

David Beckham is a very good football player. He has played for Manchester United, Real Madrid and as the captain of the England football team.

So what is it that makes David Beckham such a good footballer? 'Practise, practise, practise!' is David Beckham's motto. When he was young he would kick everything he could – footballs, tennis balls, golf balls, even cans. He was always out playing with his dad or his friends. He spent all his free time playing football.

By the time he was eight years old, David Beckham was scoring dozens of goals for his local team.

David Beckham kicking a ball

He would kick the ball and keep kicking it until he felt he was kicking really well. Then the next day he would do it all again. He was always trying to get better.

David Beckham's hero was Bryan Robson. Bryan Robson played football for England. Copying the way Bryan Robson played helped David to get better.

David's advice to young people would be to enjoy playing, enjoy kicking, enjoy the football drills, enjoy scoring and enjoy running.

Football Training Tips

1. Put your non-kicking foot beside the ball.

2. Swing your leg from your hip.

3. Kick the ball with the inside of your foot.

4. Aim at a target and try to hit it every time.

Serena Williams
Tennis Player

Serena Williams is a very good tennis player. Many people think she is the best woman tennis player in the world. Serena has won many of the top tennis **tournaments** and has also won Olympic gold medals for tennis.

So what makes Serena Williams such a good tennis player? Even though she is now one of the best players in the world, she is still trying to get even better. As well as practising her shots, she does lots of fitness training, like an athlete. All this helps her to keep improving the way she plays tennis.

Serena Williams moves into a good position to hit the ball.

She is a very **competitive** person. It does not matter what the score is, or what the weather is like, Serena Williams doesn't worry about anything other than how she is going to hit the next ball.

Serena Williams always keeps her eyes on the ball.

Tennis Training Tips

Hitting drill 1
Bounce the ball up and down on your racket lots of times. This will help you keep your eyes on the ball.

Hitting drill 2
Practise hitting against a wall. Stand sideways on to hit the ball.

Serena and her older sister Venus were both trained by their father. Their training **schedule** was very tough. They started by playing tennis together in the park when they were very young. Now both the sisters are top tennis players!

Tiger Woods
Golfer

Tiger Woods is a very good golfer. He has won many golf **tournaments** around the world. He is very **competitive**. He is the only golfer to hold all four top golfing prizes at the same time.

So what makes Tiger Woods such a good golfer? Tiger Woods has been learning to play golf since he was a baby. He used to sit in his high chair watching his father hit golf balls. When he was big enough to hold his own little golf club, he practised golf every day. Sometimes Tiger's father would interrupt and try to put him off. He was teaching him to concentrate. This was to make Tiger really think just about hitting the golf ball, not about anything else.

Tiger Woods practising his swing when he was three years old

Tiger had a hero he copied. It was Jack Nicklaus. Tiger made a chart; on it he put all the big golf **tournaments**. Then he put the age at which Jack Nicklaus won the tournaments and left a space to write the age he was when he won it.

The young Tiger Woods with his father

Golf Training Tips

1. Keep your hands together on the club.

2. As you swing the club back slowly, keep your eyes on the ball.

3. Keep your left shoulder pointing at the ball.

4. Aim to hit the bottom half of the ball.

5. If you do not have a golf club, practise with a hockey stick or a baseball bat, using a tennis ball.

6. Once you can hit the ball every time, try aiming for a target.

Ian Thorpe
Swimmer

Ian Thorpe is a very fast swimmer. He has broken over 20 world records. He has won gold medals at the Olympic Games and the World Championships. His nickname is 'Thorpedo', because he is so fast in the water – just like a **torpedo**.

So what is it that makes Ian Thorpe such a good swimmer? Ian Thorpe's motto is: 'What you put in is what you get out.' He trains hard and keeps very fit.

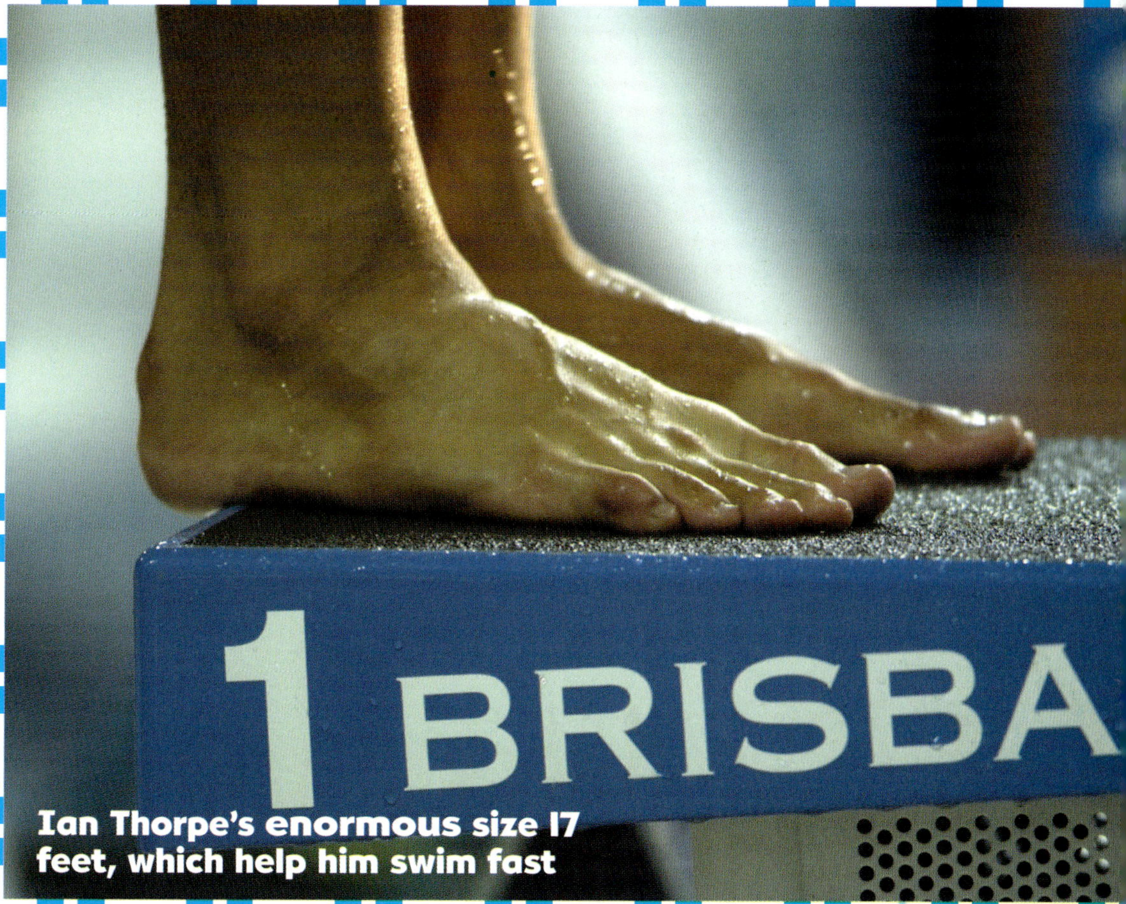

Ian Thorpe's enormous size 17 feet, which help him swim fast

Ian Thorpe is a very **determined** athlete. He gets up at 4 a.m. every morning to train. He trains as hard as he can in every session. Ian sets a time as his target, and then tries to beat that time.

Ian Thorpe's Weekly Training Schedule

Ian has ten swimming sessions a week twice a day for two hours a day.

He sleeps in on Wednesday morning. He spends Saturday afternoon and Sunday with friends and family.

Day	Swimming	Other Training
Monday	5-7.30 a.m. 4-6 p.m.	Boxing
Tuesday	5-7.30 a.m. 4-6 p.m.	Weight training
Wednesday	4-6 p.m.	
Thursday	5-7.30 a.m. 4-6 p.m.	Boxing
Friday	5-7.30 a.m. 4-6 p.m.	Weight training
Saturday	5-7.30 a.m.	
Sunday	Free	

Summary

All these people are top performers in their chosen sport. What is it that makes them stand out from the rest? What is it that helps them to succeed again and again? They all have three things in common.

Practice

All of these people started playing their sport when they were very young. They all put in hours and hours of training to get better at their sport.

Fitness

They always keep very fit. They do regular fitness training as well as playing their sport. They also eat healthy foods and drink plenty of water. This helps them to be able to keep training hard every day.

Competitiveness

Each of these athletes is very **competitive**. Each time they compete they try to do their very best. They all try to beat the records set by the performers they most admire.

Glossary

competitive – Wanting to be better than other people.

determined – With your mind firmly made up.

enormous – Very big.

schedule – A programme or timetable of planned events.

torpedo – A big, bullet-shaped weapon that goes very fast underwater.

tournament – A series of matches or competitions with a final prize.

Index